In the same series by Roland Fiddy:
The Fanatic's Guide to The Bed
The Fanatic's Guide to Cats
The Fanatic's Guide to Computers
The Fanatic's Guide to Dads
The Fanatic's Guide to Diets
The Fanatic's Guide to Dogs
The Fanatic's Guide to Golf
The Fanatic's Guide to Husbands
The Fanatic's Guide to Money
The Fanatic's Guide to Sex
The Fanatic's Guide to Skiing

First published in the USA in 1994 by Exley Giftbooks
Published in Great Britain in 1994 by Exley Publications Ltd.

Printed in Spain by GRAFO, S.A. – Bilbao.

Exley Publications Ltd, 16 Chalk Hill, Watford, Herts
WD1 4BN, United Kingdom.
Exley Giftbooks, 232 Madison Avenue, Suite 1206,
NY 10016, USA.

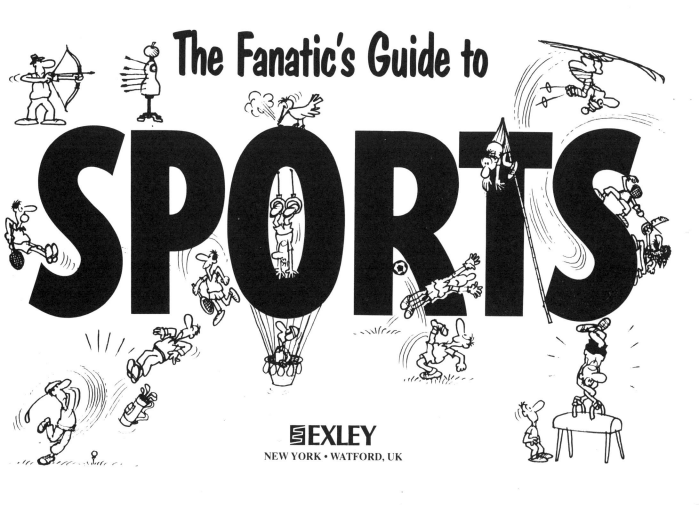

The Fanatic's Guide to SPORTS

EXLEY

NEW YORK • WATFORD, UK

What is a Sports Fanatic?

The Sports Fanatic always gives one hundred per cent effort...

A Sports Fanatic is always enthusiastic.

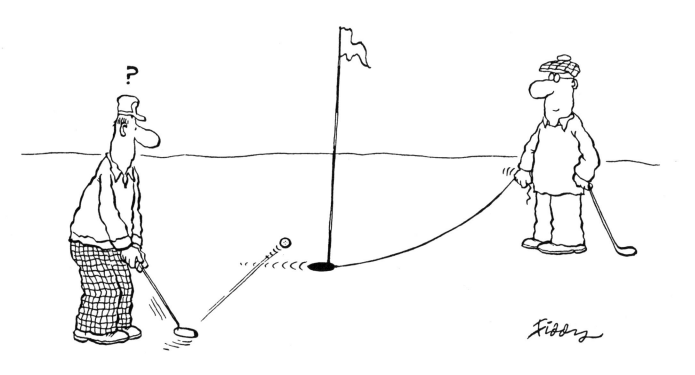

The Sports Fanatic likes to **WIN** .....

WHAT DO YOU MEAN "IT ISN'T THE END OF THE WORLD"?
UNITED
UNITED
UNITED
UNITED 1
ARSENAL 3

A Sports Fanatic should always.....

.... be aware of .....

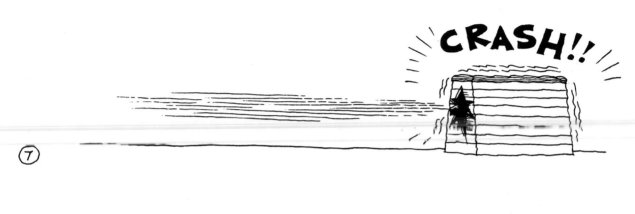

...his limitations.

①

②

①

②

⑤ ⑥ ⑦

Sports Fanatics come in all shapes.....

... and sizes .

The Sports Fanatic knows that protective gear is sometimes necessary.

The Sports Fanatic believes that one is never too old ....

... and never too young.

The Sports Fanatic is not necessarily a "Good Sport"....

BEND AND STRETCH
AND BEND AND STRETCH
AND BEND AND STRETCH....

① FINISH

②

The Sports Fanatic should always be prepared for the UNEXPECTED....

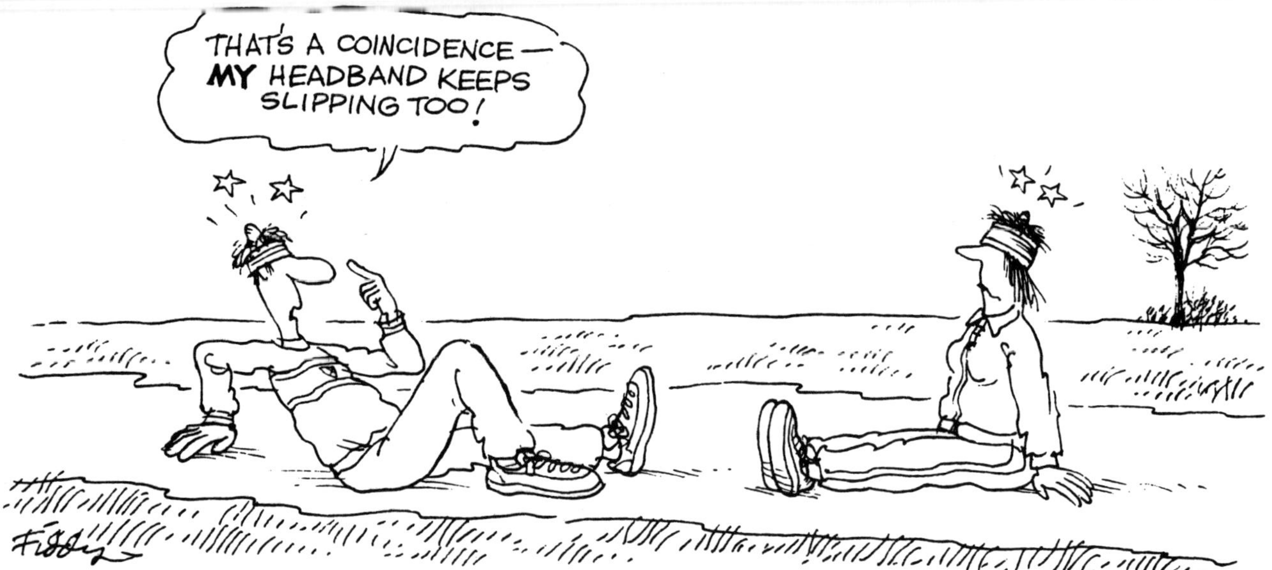
THAT'S A COINCIDENCE — MY HEADBAND KEEPS SLIPPING TOO!
Fiddy

②

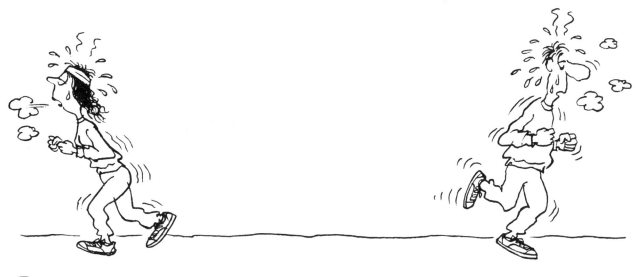

③

The Sports Fanatic appreciates the close fellowship of Team Games....

The Sports Fanatic's obsessions are not always understood by others.....

Books in the "Crazy World" series

($4.99 £2.99 paperback)

The Crazy World of Aerobics (Bill Stott)
The Crazy World of Cats (Bill Stott)
The Crazy World of Cricket (Bill Stott)
The Crazy World of Gardening (Bill Stott)
The Crazy World of Golf (Mike Scott)
The Crazy World of The Handyman (Roland Fiddy)
The Crazy World of Hospitals (Bill Stott)
The Crazy World of Housework (Bill Stott)
The Crazy World of Love (Roland Fiddy)
The Crazy World of Marriage (Bill Stott)
The Crazy World of The Office (Bill Stott)
The Crazy World of Photography (Bill Stott)
The Crazy World of Rugby (Bill Stott)
The Crazy World of Sailing (Peter Rigby)
The Crazy World of Sex (David Pye)
The Crazy World of Soccer (Bill Stott)

Books in the "Mini Joke Book" series

($6.99 £3.99 hardback)

These attractive 64 page mini joke books are illustrated throughout by Bill Stott.

A Binge of Diet Jokes
A Bouquet of Wedding Jokes
A Feast of After Dinner Jokes
A Knockout of Sports Jokes
A Portfolio of Business Jokes
A Round of Golf Jokes
A Romp of Naughty Jokes
A Spread of Over-40s Jokes
A Tankful of Motoring Jokes

Books in the "Fanatics" series

($4.99 £2.99 paperback)

The **Fanatic's Guides** are perfect presents for everyone with a hobby that has got out of hand. Eighty pages of hilarious black and white cartoons by Roland Fiddy.

The Fanatic's Guide to the Bed
The Fanatic's Guide to Cats
The Fanatic's Guide to Computers
The Fanatic's Guide to Dads
The Fanatic's Guide to Diets
The Fanatic's Guide to Dogs
The Fanatic's Guide to Husbands
The Fanatic's Guide to Money
The Fanatic's Guide to Sex
The Fanatic's Guide to Skiing

Books in the "Victim's Guide" series

($4.99 £2.99 paperback)

Award winning cartoonist Roland Fiddy sees the funny side to life's phobias, nightmares and catastrophes.

The Victim's Guide to the Baby
The Victim's Guide to the Christmas
The Victim's Guide to the Dentist
The Victim's Guide to the Doctor
The Victim's Guide to Middle Age

Great Britain: Order these super books from your local bookseller or from Exley Publications Ltd, 16 Chalk Hill, Watford, Herts WD1 4BN. (Please send £1.30 to cover postage and packing on 1 book, £2.60 on 2 or more books.)